An Introduction to the Values of the Talmud

The Complete Leader's Companion to *The Wisdom of Judaism: An Introduction to the Values of the Talmud* by Rabbi Dov Peretz Elkins

The Wisdom of Judaism
Teacher's Guide

Rabbi Dov Peretz Elkins
Winner of the National Jewish Book Award
Editor of *Yom Kippur Readings* and *Rosh Hashanah Readings*

God's To-Do List
103 Ways to Be an Angel and Do God's Work on Earth

Dr. Ron Wolfson

An inspirational guide to doing God's work in our everyday lives.

"Wolfson's pragmatic wisdom and feeling intelligence combine to add *why, how, where,* and *when* for people in search of meaning."
—Rabbi Harold M. Schulweis, founding chairman, Jewish Foundation for the Righteous

6 x 9, 144 pp, Quality Paperback, ISBN-13: 978-1-58023-301-9, ISBN-10: 1-58023-301-5

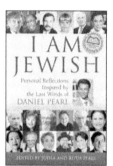

I Am Jewish
Personal Reflections Inspired by the Last Words of Daniel Pearl

Edited by Judea and Ruth Pearl

Inspires Jewish people of all backgrounds to reflect upon and take pride in their identity. Winner of the National Jewish Book Award for anthologies. Download a free copy of the *I Am Jewish Teacher's Guide* at www.jewishlights.com.

6 x 9, 304 pp, Deluxe Paperback w/flaps, ISBN-13: 978-1-58023-259-3, ISBN-10: 1-58023-259-0 Hardcover, ISBN-13: 978-1-58023-183-1, ISBN-10: 1-58023-183-7

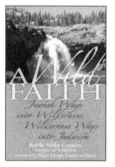

A Wild Faith
Jewish Ways into Wilderness, Wilderness Ways into Judaism

Rabbi Mike Comins; Foreword by Nigel Savage, founder of Hazon

Unravels the mystery of Judaism's connection to the natural world and offers ways to enliven and deepen spiritual life through wilderness experience. Download free copies of the Program and Study Guides at www.awildfaith.com.

6 x 9, 240 pp, Quality Paperback, ISBN-13: 978-1-58023-316-3, ISBN-10: 1-58023-316-3

Witnesses to the One
The Spiritual History of the Sh'ma

Rabbi Joseph Meszler; Foreword by Rabbi Elyse Goldstein

An exploration of Judaism's most sacred statement and world-changing idea.

"An inspiring meditation on the *Sh'ma,* filled with the resonances of Jewish history and thought....Will arouse readers to experience new dimensions of God's presence."
—Professor Susannah Heschel, Dartmouth College

6 x 9, 176 pp, Hardcover, ISBN-13: 978-1-58023-309-5, ISBN-10: 1-58023-309-0

See our website,
www.jewishlights.com,
for more information on
the momentous multivolume
My People's Prayer Book and
The Way Into... series.

An Introduction to the Values of the Talmud

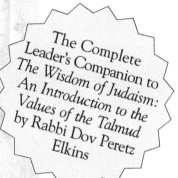

The Complete Leader's Companion to *The Wisdom of Judaism: An Introduction to the Values of the Talmud* by Rabbi Dov Peretz Elkins

The Wisdom of Judaism

Teacher's Guide

Rabbi Dov Peretz Elkins

For People of All Faiths, All Backgrounds

JEWISH LIGHTS Publishing

The Wisdom of Judaism Teacher's Guide

© 2007 by Dov Peretz Elkins

ISBN-13: 978-1-58023-350-7 (pbk.)
ISBN-13: 978-1-68336-454-2 (hardcover)

Published by Jewish Lights Publishing
www.jewishlights.com

CONTENTS

INTRODUCTION

Anyone who wants to learn more about the essential core of Judaism—the Talmud—and its elevating values and moral lessons can find meaning and satisfaction from *The Wisdom of Judaism: An Introduction to the Values of the Talmud* (Jewish Lights). The Talmud is referred to as a sea in the pages of rabbinic literature because its contents are so vast, comprehensive, and all-encompassing, stretching from distant point to distant point. The phrase *Yam HaTalmud* (Sea of the Talmud) accurately describes the massive amount of legal, historical, allegorical, and ethical material that it covers. Further, chronologically the Talmudic period spans some six or seven centuries of rabbinic thought, discussion, dialogue, and teaching.

I like to use an additional metaphor to describe the contents of the Talmud. It is not only a sea, but it can be seen as an endless forest. As in all forests, there are beautiful flowers, magnificent trees, unusual bushes, a rainbow of colors, smells, and tastes, harmonious and also cacophonous sounds. But also as in a forest, you can easily get scratched, bruised, or lost, if not careful. The purpose of putting together the maxims of the rabbinic period in *The Wisdom of Judaism* is to provide a guidebook for those new to the Talmud so that they can find the splashes of beauty and variegated colors, rather than slip and fall on the broken branches and hidden obstacles that may lurk unseen, and cause harm or hurt, or, more likely, meaningless meandering.

With you as their tour guide, this Teacher's Guide will help you get your students to see the deeper meaning of Talmudic literature and the great insights of our ancient rabbinic sages. Classes of teens, adults, or seniors can tackle the questions and discuss their answers together or in small groups. Following the structure of the book, the lessons in this Guide are:

- "Kindness through Giving, Welcoming, and Sharing"
- "Human Relationships: Treating Others Fairly, Openly, and Lovingly"
- "Personal Values through Humility, Awareness, and Dignity"
- "Family Values: Living Respectfully with Mates, Children, and Parents"

- "Teaching and Learning: Methods, Goals, and Results"
- "Life's Puzzles: A Potpourri of Solutions to Everyday Problems"

You may request that students read a certain portion of *The Wisdom of Judaism* before class. At the beginning of your session, you can jump-start the conversation by displaying the quote that introduces each section of this Guide and leading a discussion based on the text and questions that follow. Just as each part of the book is an independent unit, so are these lessons, which means you do not have to use every lesson or assign the sections in order, but cover them in the manner that best suits the needs of your class.

As your students begin their exploration of the Talmud, I hope that *The Wisdom of Judaism*—and the thoughtful questions in this Guide—help them avoid the potential pitfalls and mistaken pathways, and discover the flowers and the fruits.

I

Kindness through Giving, Welcoming, and Sharing

Words of Torah

"Deeds of kindness are equal to all the commandments."

Talmud Yerushalmi, Tractate Peah 1:1

Questions for Discussion

Jewish tradition has strongly emphasized the quality of kindness. This is expressed in many different ways—such as tzedakah (charity), hospitality, compassion, sensitivity—as is shown in the first part of the book. Let's explore the ways Judaism manifests its rules for kind behavior by tackling these questions:

1. What does Martin Buber, the Austrian-Israeli philosopher, mean by saying that the way to approach the divine is through "becoming human" (p. 4)? What other ways do you think are available to us to approach the divine?

2. The statement from Avot (1:5)—"Let the doors of your home be wide open, and may the needy be often in your home" (p. 7)—includes hospitality to all people, but especially to the needy. Why do you think Jews have historically been exemplary in the practices of hospitality and charity?

3. Do you distinguish between giving to Jewish charities and to secular charities? Why or why not?

4. Do you think you should give tzedakah even when an emotional component, such as feelings of caring and concern, is absent? Explain your views.

5. Do you think that humans are wired to act kindly, or is kindness a quality that needs to be taught (nature vs. nurture)?

6. As stated in Y'vamot 79a, three qualities define the Jewish people: "They are compassionate, they are modest, and they perform acts of lovingkindness" (p. 15). How have Jews historically, as a whole, fulfilled the charge to carry out these three noble qualities? Which one has been carried out most prominently? Which needs additional attention in our lives today?

7. How does your community treat intermarried Jews? How do you feel about it? What can be done today to be more welcoming to intermarried couples?

8. Why do the Rabbis consider shaming a human being as equal to murder?

9. How does treating animals well foster respect for all living creatures?

II

Human Relationships:
Treating Others Fairly, Openly, and Lovingly

Words of Torah

> "Rabbi Simlai declared, 'The Torah begins and ends
> with acts of lovingkindness.'"

Sotah 14a

Questions for Discussion

Getting along with others can be challenging. At times we struggle in all our relationships—even with (and sometimes especially with) our best friends, our family, and our co-workers. The Talmudic wisdom in Part II of *The Wisdom of Judaism* offers much advice in this regard. Let's now examine some of the issues connected with interpersonal relationships.

1. Why do you think the ancient Rabbis focus so much of their writing on the relationships between human beings?
2. What are the benefits and detriments of moderation when it comes to our relationships?
3. What are some of the obstacles you might face in turning an enemy into a friend? How can they be overcome?
4. In what ways does Judaism stress the importance of community? Why is community stressed to such an extent? How important is community in your own life?

5. Do you sustain relationships with people with whom you rarely discuss serious matters? What are the benefits of maintaining such relationships? What are the differences between relationships such as these, and relationships with people with whom the conversation is more serious?

6. How does the Jewish emphasis on justice, equality, and democracy manifest itself in Jewish community life?

7. Why do you think it's so easy to focus on the things we want to change in others, and so difficult to recognize the things we need to change in ourselves?

8. What are the best conditions with which to convey feedback to someone, to make it possible and more likely that the other will hear and accept it?

9. Do you believe it is ever okay to engage in behaviors while alone that you wouldn't ever do in front of people? Why or why not? What role does the belief that God is always present play in your answer? Do you believe God is always present?

III

Personal Values through Humility, Awareness, and Dignity

Words of Torah

"Your own conduct will command respect for you."

Tractate Eduyot 9b

Questions for Discussion

The Talmud contains many tractates filled with honest debate and struggle about how to live a life that is worthy and moral, to achieve the highest possible values. Part III deals with many of these noble personal and corporate values, such as peace, equality, humility, flexibility, self-reliance, and human dignity. Let's discuss how they influence our lives.

1. Throughout history many great thinkers have tried to explain the source of the countless wars that constantly dot the pages of human chronicles. What are some of the reasons why there are always so many wars going on in the world? What can we do to diminish or eliminate them?

2. What is the relationship between sharing grief and sharing joy and relief? Why does the former seem to be a prerequisite for the latter?

3. In what ways does a system of public justice that is recognized as fair and equitable affect the morale of a community? What happens to a community when the system is corrupt?

4. One of the most difficult qualities a person can develop is humility. Why is that the case?

5. In what ways does Jewish historical experience affect the rabbinical statement that one should "choose to be persecuted rather than persecute another" (p. 71)?

6. Share a few examples in which the quality of flexibility helped to solve a thorny problem—in relationships, at work, or in other circumstances—in your life.

7. Many religious and cultural traditions encourage their adherents to "live in the now" (see pp. 77–79). Why does it sometimes seem easier to live in the past or dream of the future, instead of being "in the now"?

8. Why would the Rabbis of the Talmud stress reliance as a virtue more important than keeping the Sabbath? How can we help others to be self-reliant?

9. Jews are mostly associated with mental labor—intellectual challenge, debate, study, and the like. Why do you think that the value of physical labor is extolled in the Talmud (pp. 82–84)?

IV

Family Values: Living Respectfully with Mates, Children, and Parents

Words of Torah

"One who teaches Torah to children abides with the divine presence."

Bava Metzia 85

Questions for Discussion

Jewish tradition places great emphasis on family values. Many people who are born in other faith traditions and choose to become Jewish do so because of the strength of the Jewish family. Part IV focuses on the historical vigor of Jewish family relationships, which we'll now discuss.

1. What are the greatest challenges in maintaining a marriage or committed union? What are some characteristics of a partnership that lasts?

2. Do you find it more difficult to sustain very close relationships than those that are less intimate? Why or why not?

3. Explain what this sentence means: "The best way to honor God is to honor all who are God's children" (p. 95).

4. How does economics enter into the stability of a family relationship?

5. What would you consider some of the weaknesses of your upbringing? If the influence of our home environment exerts such a strong impact on

the rest of our lives, how can we rise above the weaknesses we experienced in our earliest years?

6. What do you think about the fact that one has to study, practice, and take a difficult test to obtain a driver's license, yet anyone can sign on the dotted line and get a marriage license?

7. We all know people who are perfectly happy living a single life. Why do the Rabbis put such strong emphasis on sharing one's life with a spouse/companion?

8. What suggestions do you have to bridge the "generation gap"? Why is it important for older and younger folks to communicate with, and have respect for, one another?

9. What makes it so difficult to achieve what is called "unconditional love," love that is not dependent on a motive (pp. 109–110)?

V

Teaching and Learning: Methods, Goals, and Results

Words of Torah

"The study of the Torah is more important than the rebuilding of the Temple in Jerusalem."

Megillah 16b

Questions for Discussion

Long before most other peoples, the Jews placed significant emphasis on the importance of study and learning. From centuries of experience, Jewish teachers and educators have drawn important conclusions about the learning process. Let's come to some of our own conclusions.

1. When we conjure an image of a traditional yeshivah, an academy of study, we see pairs of students poring over holy texts hour after hour. What made it important throughout the ages to spend such lengthy periods of time in Torah study?

2. Describe an occasion when you taught or explained an idea or a skill to another person. From this experience, do you agree that teaching something to others is the best way to learn yourself (pp. 116–118)? Why or why not?

3. The Jerusalem Talmud argues that a nation's strongest assets are moral rather than military (pp. 119–120). Explain why you may agree or disagree with this point of view.

4. What are some of the ways we can teach our Jewish values to our children and grandchildren so that they are interested, engaged, and prepared to pass the same values on to *their* children and grandchildren?

5. We have all heard of people who scrupulously follow the ritual details of their tradition, and yet have a very shallow understanding of its intellectual basis. Why does the Talmud have such a strong aversion for such a person?

6. The Rabbis suggest that "the less a person knows, the more he or she talks" (p. 129). What acts of diplomacy and discretion can prevent a meeting from being dominated by those with little knowledge?

7. Why does it state in Pirke Avot that "an ignoramus cannot be pious" (p. 132)? What does this statement mean?

8. The ancient Rabbis believed that a certain level of innate intelligence is a prerequisite for deep learning. Explain why you agree or disagree with this point of view.

VI

Life's Puzzles: A Potpourri of Solutions to Everyday Problems

Words of Torah

"God created the evil inclination, but also the Torah as the antidote."

Bava Batra 16a

Questions for Discussion

Since religious life has been the central axis of the Jewish people from its very beginnings, it is not surprising that the Talmud grapples with such a wide variety of complex theological and human issues, such as defining miracles, balancing ethics and ritual, the definition of authentic spiritual leadership, and so on. These are some of the topics we will wrestle with in this lesson.

1. How do you define a miracle?
2. Pages 142–144 discuss the connection between effort and reward. How do you explain the fact that sometimes people who put forth no effort at all are rewarded?
3. The Rabbis suggest that sincerity in religious practice is more important than the amount of rituals one performs. Obviously the Rabbis were not suggesting that people can do the very minimum in all cases as long as what they do is sincere. What do you think their intention is in this matter?
4. What role does emotion play in religious life?

5. What are the most effective ways to establish life goals that are realistic and reachable?

6. The phrase "wounded healer" has entered our modern vocabulary in the healing and other professions. It seems to imply that most leaders have their own foibles and weaknesses. How can people with their own faults help the rest of us, if they themselves are not perfect?

7. Why is it sometimes difficult for people with authority to exercise their influence in a fair way? How does one balance power with equity?

8. Why is it so difficult for some people to admit ignorance? What might be some of the consequences of failing to do so? How can we become more comfortable with our own shortcomings and limits?

9. What are our obligations to God? What are our obligations to our fellow humans? How can we balance the two?

Rabbi Dov Peretz Elkins, a lecturer, educator and author, is rabbi emeritus of The Jewish Center of Princeton, New Jersey, and a former member of the Committee on Jewish Law and Standards of the Rabbinical Assembly and the Council for Jewish Education. He has written widely for the Jewish and general press and is also the editor of *Yom Kippur Readings: Inspiration, Information and Contemplation* and *Rosh Hashanah Readings: Inspiration, Information and Contemplation* (both Jewish Lights Publishing). His website is www.wisdomofjudaism.org.

Other Books by Rabbi Dov Peretz Elkins

 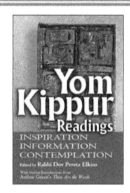

Rosh Hashanah Readings
Inspiration, Information and Contemplation

6 x 9, 400 pp, Hardcover
ISBN-13: 978-1-58023-239-5, ISBN-10: 1-58023-239-6

Yom Kippur Readings
Inspiration, Information and Contemplation

6 x 9, 368 pp, Hardcover
ISBN-13: 978-1-58023-271-5, ISBN-10: 1-58023-271-X

Drawn from a variety of sources—ancient, medieval, modern, Jewish and non-Jewish—these selections of readings, prayers and insights explore the opportunities for inspiration and reflection inherent in the themes addressed on the High Holy Days.

Praise for the Work of Rabbi Dov Peretz Elkins

"His choice of text is solid, his commentary insightful, and his style is both enlightening and engaging."
—**Rabbi Rami Shapiro,** author, *Ethics of the Sages:* Pirke Avot—*Annotated & Explained*

"Filled with inspirational readings that are profound, and that will challenge and ignite the mind and heart alike.... Will deepen the High Holy Day experience for every reader."
—**Rabbi Joseph Telushkin,** author, *Jewish Literacy* and *The Book of Jewish Values*

"Clearly and beautifully elucidates important teachings on spiritual concepts like love, charity, kindness and companionship—plus some of life's sticky issues like greed, sin, and belief. A great book for anyone wanting to dip into the pool of Judaism's timeless wisdom."
—**Rabbi Elyse Goldstein,** editor, *The Women's Torah Commentary* and *The Women's Haftarah Commentary*

For People of All Faiths, All Backgrounds

JEWISH LIGHTS Publishing
www.jewishlights.com

Printed in the USA
CPSIA information can be obtained
at www.ICGtesting.com
JSHW060049150824
68134JS00031B/2700